NATIONAL GEOGRAPHIC

T0045521

Potatoes

Beatrice Duggan

Did you know that farmers plant potatoes in the ground?
New potatoes grow from these old potatoes.

Farmers use machines to plant potatoes. They plant the potatoes in rows.

MF
EVC 211Y

New potato plants grow from the old potatoes that were planted. The plants are green and leafy.

Flowers grow on the potato plants.
Potatoes grow under the ground.

Farmers use a machine to pick the potatoes. They send the potatoes to stores.

We buy the potatoes to eat. Yum!